I0796603
All about TRUCKS
GMC TRUCKS
By Evangelene Alaraj
AV2
www.av2books.com

Step 1
Go to **www.av2books.com**

Step 2
Enter this unique code
PHVBQB1OF

Step 3
Explore your interactive eBook!

AV2 is optimized for use on any device

Your interactive eBook comes with...

Contents
Browse a live contents page to easily navigate through resources

Audio
Listen to sections of the book read aloud

Videos
Watch informative video clips

Weblinks
Gain additional information for research

Slideshows
View images and captions

Try This!
Complete activities and hands-on experiments

Key Words
Study vocabulary, and complete a matching word activity

Quizzes
Test your knowledge

Share
Share titles within your Learning Management System (LMS) or Library Circulation System

Citation
Create bibliographical references following the Chicago Manual of Style

This title is part of our AV2 digital subscription

1-Year 3–8 Subscription
ISBN 978-1-7911-3306-1

Access hundreds of AV2 titles with our digital subscription.
Sign up for a FREE trial at **www.av2books.com/trial**

GMC TRUCKS

CONTENTS

GMC
485·ZEN

GMC TRUCKS

The pickup truck of today has style and function. Its **interior** is spacious and comfortable, while its **exterior** is strong and sturdy. A pickup truck can be a family vehicle for sports events and vacations. It can also do heavy-duty jobs, such as towing a trailer. More than 100 years of engineering have made this possible. The stylish, mega-powered trucks of today come from a long history of inventions.

In 1911, General Motors created GMC, a truck company. The company's first trucks were not just pickups. GMC built delivery and fire truck models to help American cities grow. It also designed military trucks to carry soldiers during World War I and World War II. Newer and better pickup truck models were soon to follow.

General Motors is the **largest automaker** in the United States.

GMC is General Motors' **third-largest brand** globally.

In **2020**, GMC sold **253,016** Sierra pickup trucks in the United States.

WILLIAM C. DURANT

"The automotive industry is and will continue to be an essential factor in the development of our whole civilization." -William C. Durant

William C. Durant was a talented salesman. He was confident and liked to take risks. One of his early business **ventures** was with an older style of transportation, horse-drawn carriages. Durant and a partner made carriages in a factory in Flint, Michigan. The building is now called Factory One. It was the birthplace of both General Motors and GMC trucks.

Durant realized that cars and trucks would soon replace carriages. However, he was an **entrepreneur**, not an inventor. Unable to design his own models, he looked for automakers he could buy. In 1908, he formed General Motors from 13 car companies and 10 factories.

Durant believed that automobiles were key to the future. He formed other auto companies after founding General Motors.

MAPPING GMC TODAY

Both GMC and its parent company, General Motors, are headquartered in Detroit, Michigan.

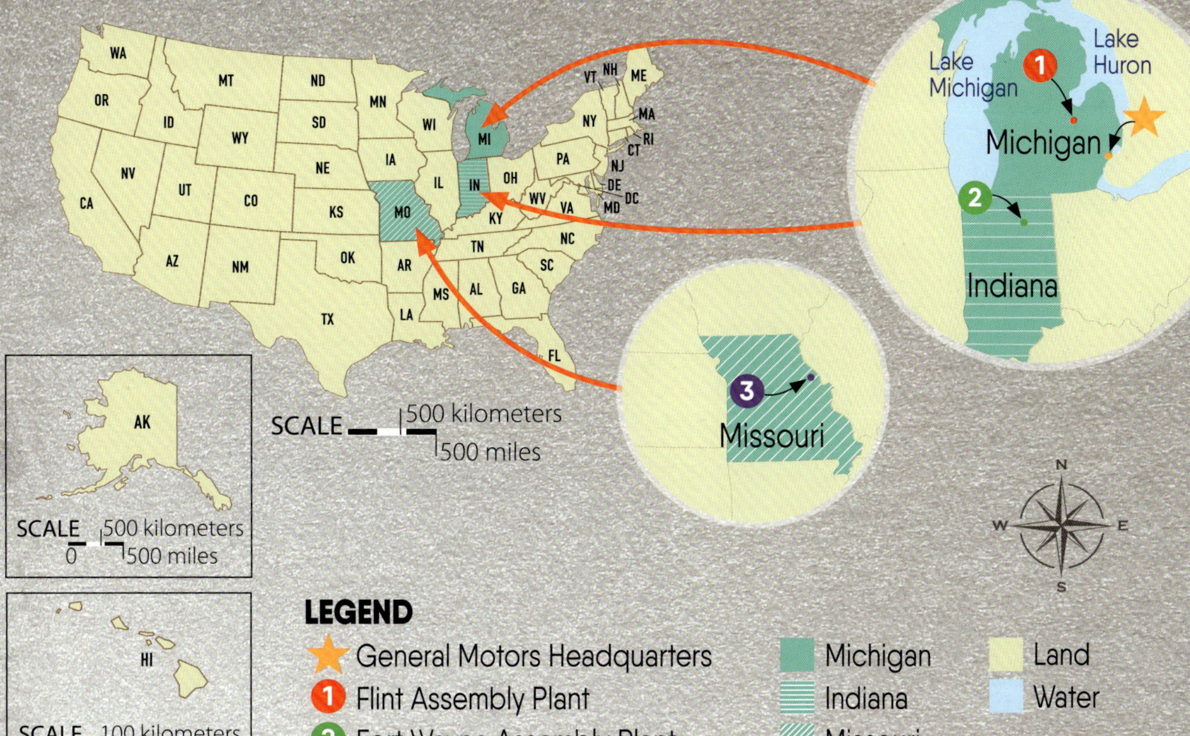

LEGEND

- General Motors Headquarters
- 1 Flint Assembly Plant
- 2 Fort Wayne Assembly Plant
- 3 Wentzville Assembly Plant
- Michigan
- Indiana
- Missouri
- Land
- Water

1 *Flint Assembly Plant* Flint, Michigan

Current products: GMC Sierra
Year opened: 1947
Site size: 159 acres (64 hectares)
People employed: 5,434

2 *Fort Wayne Assembly Plant* Roanoke, Indiana

Current products: GMC Sierra
Year opened: 1986
Site size: 716 acres (290 ha)
People employed: 4,424

3 *Wentzville Assembly Plant* Wentzville, Missouri

Current products: GMC Canyon
Year opened: 1983
Site size: 569 acres (230 ha)
People employed: 3,764

THE LOGO

The first GMC **emblem** had decorative white letters. A black background made the letters stand out. The words "General Motors Trucks" filled an orange outer circle. GMC used this design until 1947.

There have been only three major emblem changes in the company's history. The current emblem has been in use since 1966. It has had only minor updates since then.

GMC EMBLEM

Big red letters have been part of GMC's emblem since 1966.

Silver rims and bold, straight letters replaced more decorative designs in 1966.

General Motors chose a simple design to represent the power and utility of GMC trucks. The design looks similar to the strong curves and bright sheen of paint on a new pickup truck.

GMC THROUGH HISTORY

The first trucks to feature the GMC emblem were not made by GMC. They were Rapid and Reliance electric trucks. GMC trucks began using the GMC logo soon after, and they have used it ever since.

1911

General Motors organizes the General Motors Truck Company to sell gas and electric truck models. The "GMC" trade name is first used in August.

1916

A GMC truck becomes the first vehicle to cross the United States in less than 32 days. It travels from Seattle to New York City.

1930s

GMC's production drops sharply during the **Great Depression**. The company slowly begins recovering in 1933.

During World War II, GMC builds 600,000 trucks with six-cylinder power "Army Workhorse Engines" for the U.S. military.

A fully electric "supertruck" called the Hummer EV joins GMC's lineup.

1940s **2014** **2021**

An all-new EcoTec3 engine debuts in GMC's best-selling Sierra line.

GMC SIERRA

The Sierra is GMC's best-selling pickup truck. It has been a popular model since its release in 1988. The name comes from the Spanish *sierra*, which means "mountain range." Like a mountain range, the Sierra is considered both attractive and powerful. GMC had previously used the name for trim options, which are features that offer greater power, styling, and comfort. The Sierra line continues to offer many of these deluxe features.

Thanks to the Sierra line, GMC had one of the best years in its sales history in 2019.

The 2021 GMC Sierra has an illuminated emblem that comes in black or red.

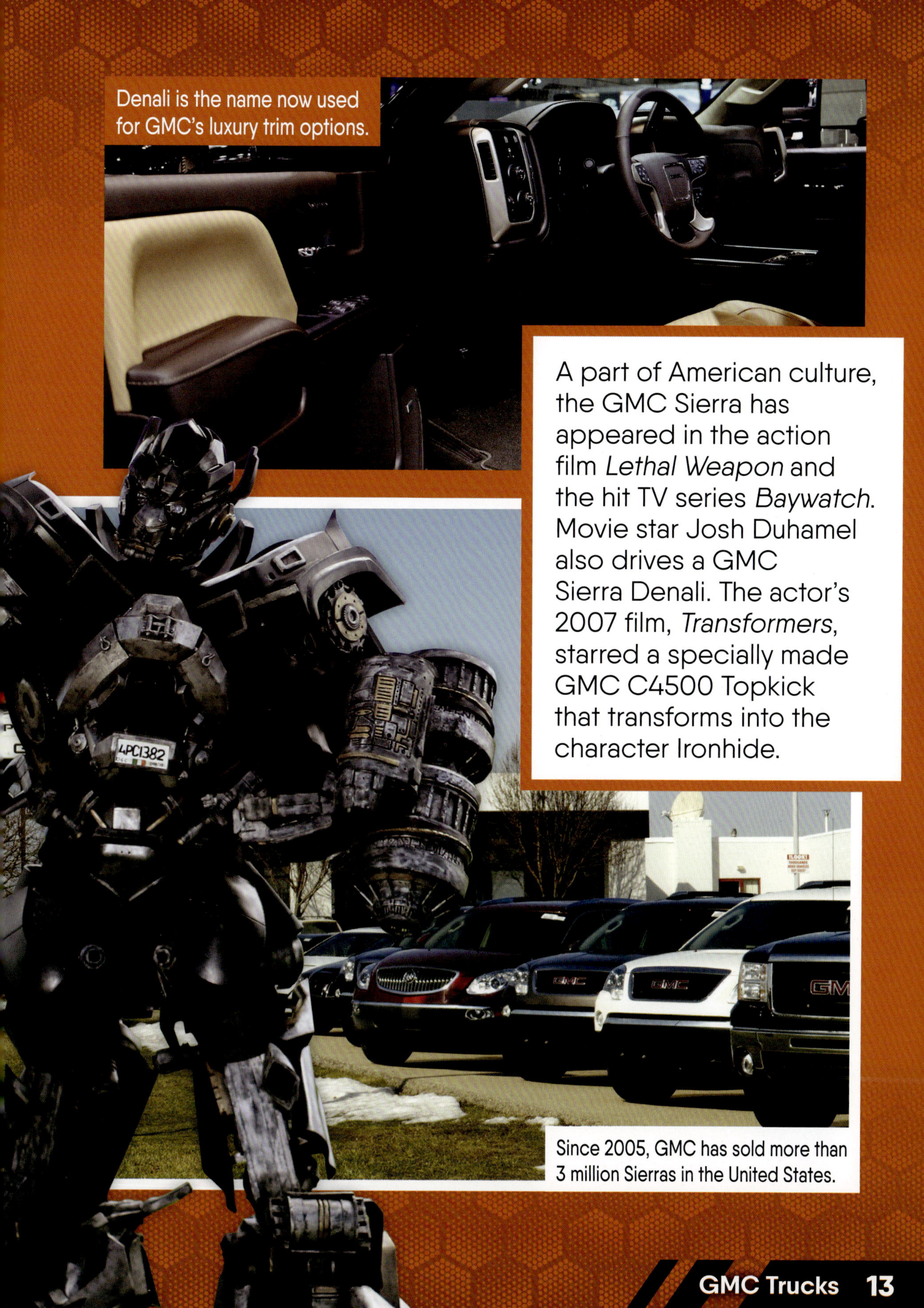

Denali is the name now used for GMC's luxury trim options.

A part of American culture, the GMC Sierra has appeared in the action film *Lethal Weapon* and the hit TV series *Baywatch*. Movie star Josh Duhamel also drives a GMC Sierra Denali. The actor's 2007 film, *Transformers*, starred a specially made GMC C4500 Topkick that transforms into the character Ironhide.

Since 2005, GMC has sold more than 3 million Sierras in the United States.

"LIKE A PRO"

GMC's recent **slogan**, "Like a Pro," promises high standards and well-made vehicles. Pickup truck designs need to be suitable for hard-working professionals. Drivers expect to have all the latest technological improvements that will help them be successful.

GMC has added many professional touches to its trucks in recent years. Surround-view cameras show all sides of the truck. Sensors detect bumps on the road and react as needed, allowing for a smoother driving experience. The 2019 Sierra Denali also introduced the MultiPro **tailgate**. This tailgate can be folded into six different positions.

Since 2015, all GMC models have included a 4G Wi-Fi hotspot.

GMC used its "We Are Professional Grade" slogan for nearly 20 years.

Select GMC models now have a built-in Alexa app.

HOW IT'S MADE

General Motors has 11 assembly plants in the United States. Some of these plants build GMC trucks. The Fort Wayne Assembly Plant in Roanoke, Indiana, builds GMC Sierra regular and extended **cabs**. A regular cab has two doors and one row of seating. Extended cabs may have a bench or foldable seats at the back. Some extended cabs also have a set of shorter side doors. Crew cabs are the largest **configuration**. They have four full-sized doors and can seat up to six people.

Assembling a truck is a complicated process with many steps. Multiple robots work on each truck.

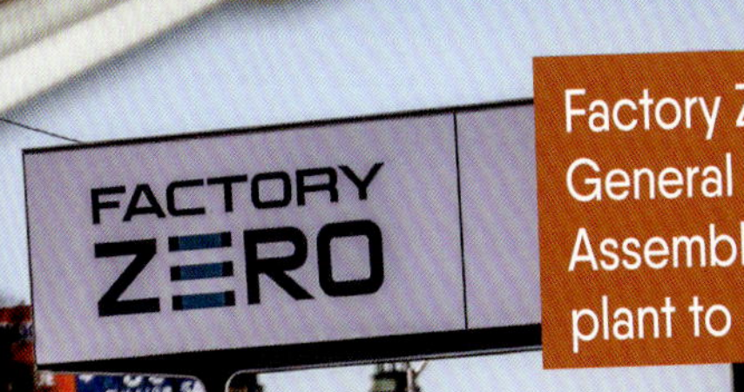

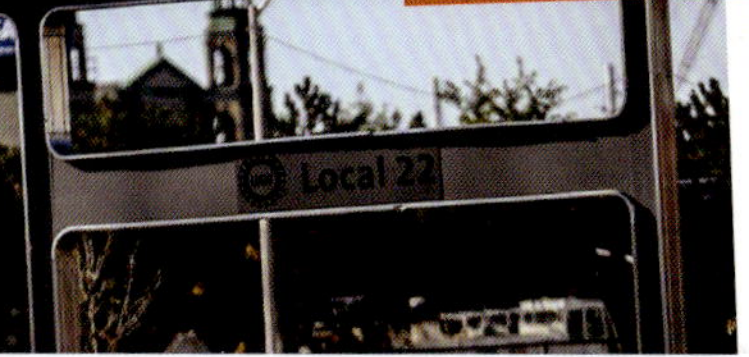

Factory ZERO is the new name of General Motors' Detroit-Hamtramck Assembly Plant. It will be the first plant to make only electric vehicles.

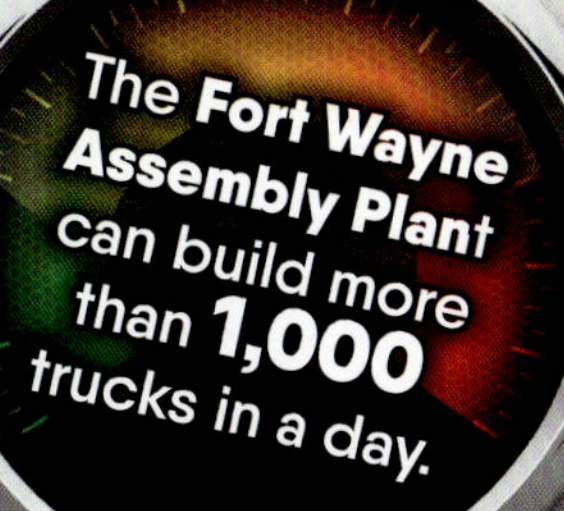

The Fort Wayne Assembly Plant is one of the busiest automobile assembly plants in the United States.

The **Fort Wayne Assembly Plant** can build more than **1,000** trucks in a day.

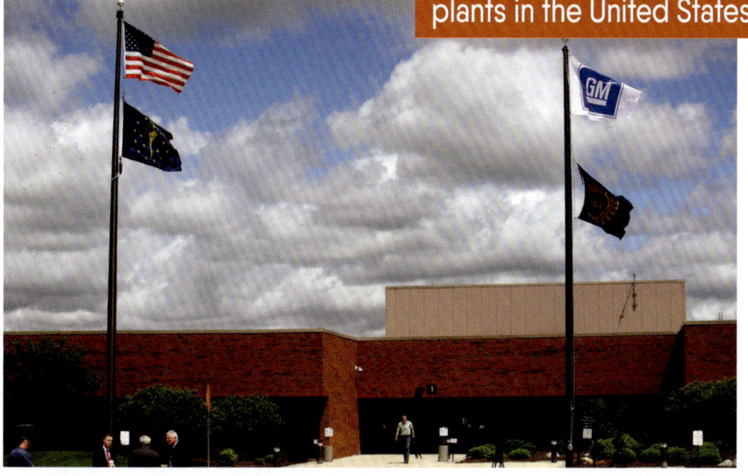

GMC sold **515,311** vehicles in the United States in **2020**.

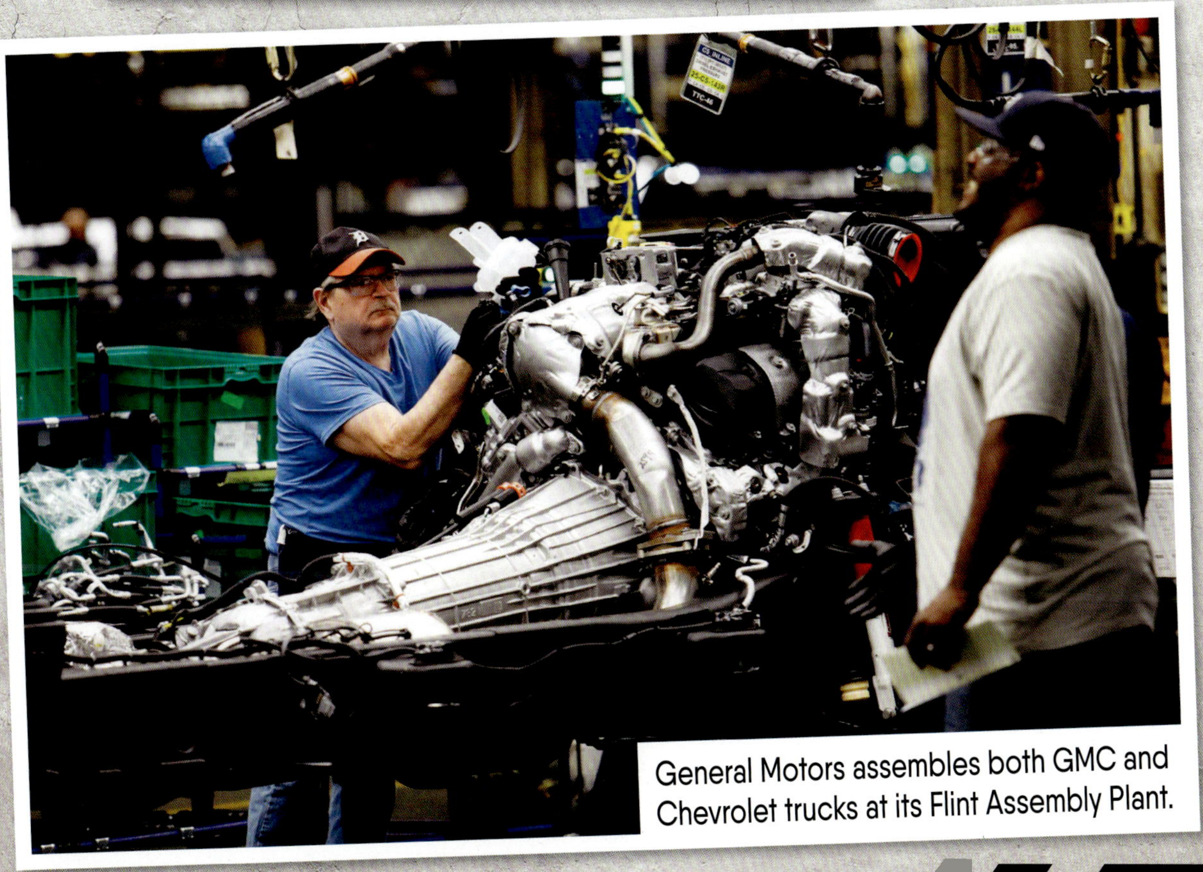

General Motors assembles both GMC and Chevrolet trucks at its Flint Assembly Plant.

TODAY'S LINEUP

GMC trucks are popular in the United States, Canada, and the Middle East. The company's Canyon line is a light-duty, affordable option. Light-duty means that a truck has a lower **towing capacity** than medium-duty or heavy-duty trucks. The amount a truck can tow depends on engine power and accessories, such as **hitches**. Today, GMC builds mostly light-duty and heavy-duty pickups.

Here are some of the GMC trucks on the road today.

GMC GMC Canyon

Engine: **2.5L 4-cylinder**

Horsepower: **200**

Maximum Towing Capacity: **7,700 pounds** (3,500 kg)

Starting Price: **$26,800**

GMC GMC Sierra 1500

Engine: **4.3L V6**

Horsepower: **285**

Maximum Towing Capacity: **11,800 pounds** (5,400 kg)

Starting Price: **$30,100**

GMC Canyon Denali

Engine: **3.6L V6**

Horsepower: **308**

Maximum Towing Capacity:
7,550 pounds (3,400 kg)

Starting Price: **$41,200**

GMC Sierra 1500 Denali

Engine: **5.3L V8**

Horsepower: **355**

Maximum Towing Capacity:
9,200 pounds (4,200 kg)

Starting Price: **$55,800**

GMC Sierra 2500 HD AT4

Engine: **6.6L V8**

Horsepower: **401**

Maximum Towing Capacity:
18,500 pounds (8,400 kg)

Starting Price: **$59,100**

TOMORROW'S GMC

The Hummer EV is ready to enter GMC's lineup as "The World's First All-Electric Supertruck." It will use only electricity to run. The Hummer EV recharges quickly. This model can charge 100 miles (160 kilometers) of power in only 10 minutes. GMC calls the truck a "quiet revolution." The Hummer EV will be a large off-roading vehicle, but it will have the quiet power of electricity.

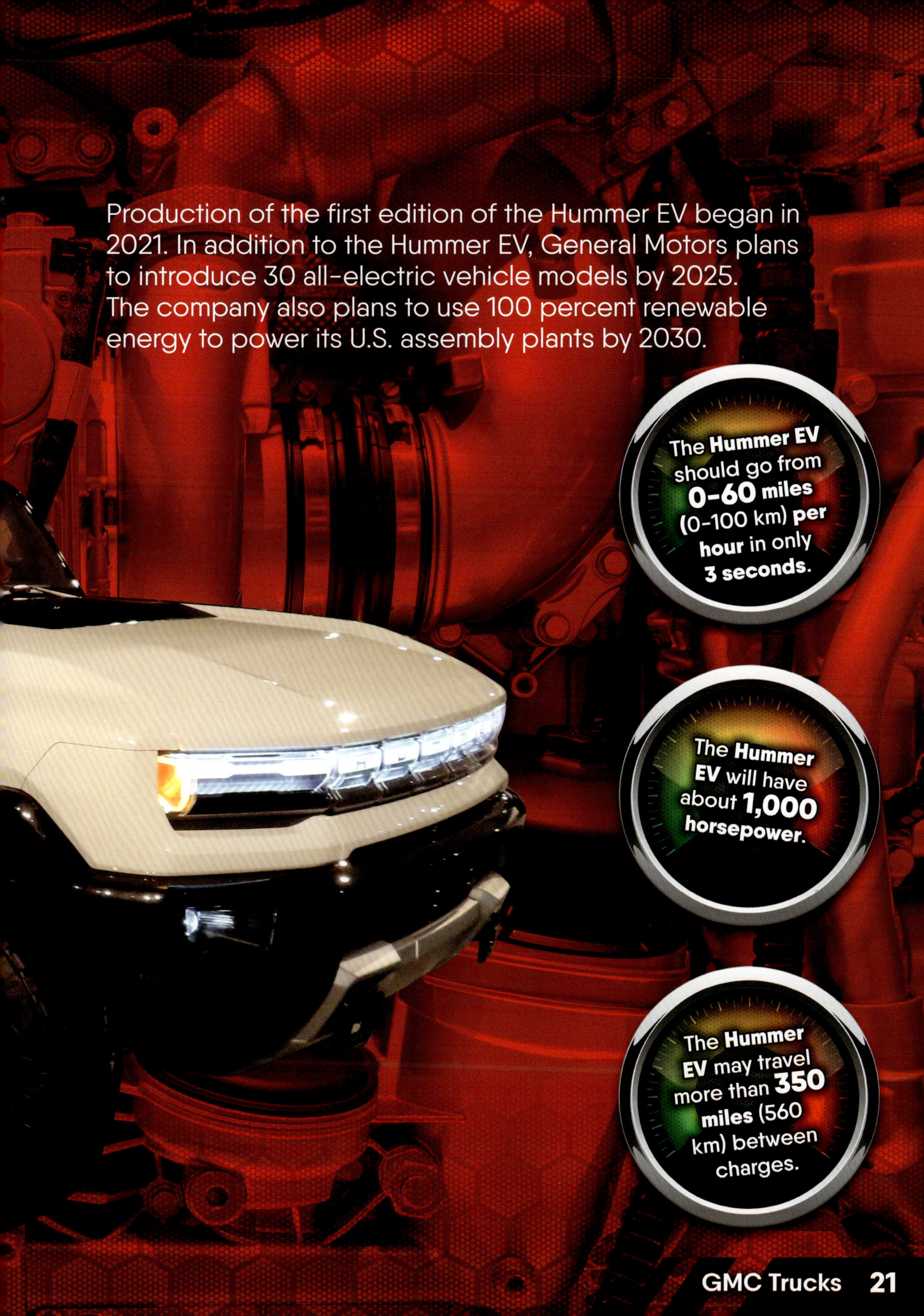

Production of the first edition of the Hummer EV began in 2021. In addition to the Hummer EV, General Motors plans to introduce 30 all-electric vehicle models by 2025. The company also plans to use 100 percent renewable energy to power its U.S. assembly plants by 2030.

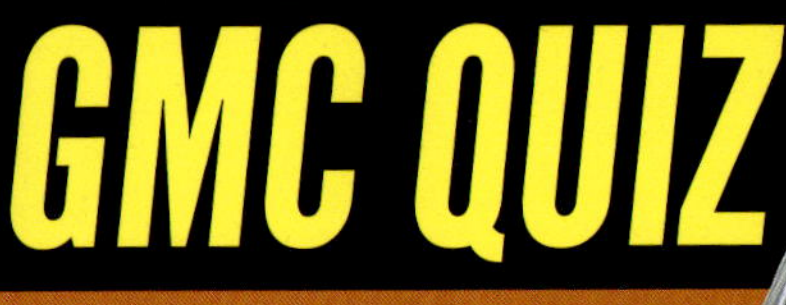

1 When did General Motors create GMC?

2 Who formed General Motors?

3 What is the Detroit-Hamtramck plant's new name?

4 How many military trucks did GMC build during World War II?

5 What does the word *sierra* mean?

6 Which *Transformers* character did a GMC C4500 Topkick transform into?

7 How many trucks can the Fort Wayne plant build in a day?

8 What is GMC's current slogan?

9 What is the name of GMC's all-new, fully electric truck?

10 How many electric vehicles does GMC plan to introduce by 2025?

ANSWERS

1. 1911 **2.** William C. Durant
3. Factory ZERO **4.** 600,000
5. "Mountain range" **6.** Ironhide
7. More than 1,000 **8.** "Like a Pro"
9. The Hummer EV **10.** 30

KEY WORDS

cabs: the front parts of trucks where drivers sit

configuration: design or layout of a truck

emblem: letters or small images on a vehicle that represent the company that made it

entrepreneur: a person who starts new companies

exterior: outside area

Great Depression: the long and severe economic downturn of the 1930s

hitches: the connectors between vehicles and the objects they tow

interior: inside area

slogan: a short, catchy phrase that a company uses to define its brands

tailgate: a door at the back of a truck or car, hinged at the bottom so that it opens downwards

towing capacity: the amount of weight a vehicle can pull

venture: a financially risky project

INDEX

Get the best of both worlds.

AV2 bridges the gap between print and digital.

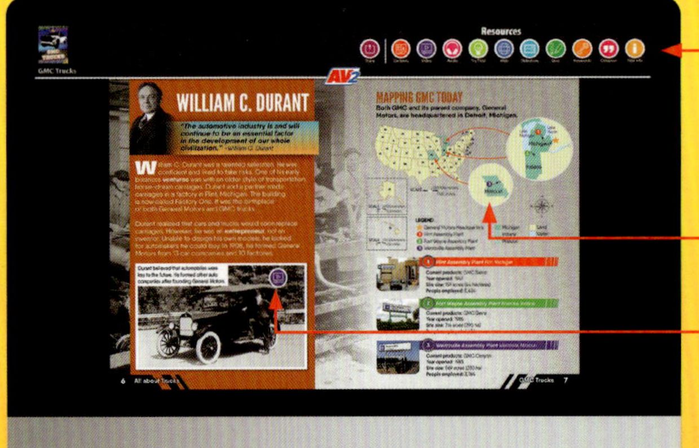

The expandable resources toolbar enables quick access to content including **videos**, **audio**, **activities**, **weblinks**, **slideshows**, **quizzes**, and **key words**.

Animated videos make static images come alive.

Resource icons on each page help readers to further **explore key concepts**.

Published by AV2
276 5th Avenue, Suite 704 #917
New York, NY 10001
Website: www.av2books.com

Library of Congress Cataloging-in-Publication Data

Names: Alaraj, Evangelene, author.
Title: GMC trucks / Evangelene Alaraj.
Description: New York, NY : AV2, [2022] | Series: All about trucks | Includes index. | Audience: Ages 8-12. | Audience: Grades 2-3.
Identifiers: LCCN 2021023301 (print) | LCCN 2021023302 (ebook) | ISBN 9781791141875 (library binding) | ISBN 9781791141882 (paperback) | ISBN 9781791141899
Subjects: LCSH: GMC trucks--Juvenile literature.
Classification: LCC TL230.5.G57 A44 2021 (print) | LCC TL230.5.G57 (ebook) | DDC 629.223/2--dc23
LC record available at https://lccn.loc.gov/2021023301
LC ebook record available at https://lccn.loc.gov/2021023302

Printed in Guangzhou, China
1 2 3 4 5 6 7 8 9 0 25 24 23 22 21

072021
101120

Art Director: Terry Paulhus **Project Coordinator:** Priyanka Das

Every reasonable effort has been made to trace ownership and to obtain permission to reprint copyright material. The publisher would be pleased to have any errors or omissions brought to its attention so that they may be corrected in subsequent printings.

The publisher acknowledges Alamy, Getty Images, Shutterstock, and Wikimedia as its primary image suppliers for this title.